Bridget, Gabi,
Owen, Colette,
Here's a great
way to talk to God!

He will know
what you find
important in this
world, and what
you are grateful
for!   Love,
       Grandma
       March 26, 2010
       XX OO
       XX OO

PRAYER
FOR A CHILD

BY RACHEL FIELD
PICTURES BY ELIZABETH ORTON JONES

Simon & Schuster Books for Young Readers

SIMON & SCHUSTER BOOKS FOR YOUNG READERS
An imprint of Simon & Schuster Children's Publishing Division
1230 Avenue of the Americas, New York, New York 10020

Manufactured in China

Library of Congress Cataloging-in-Publication
Field, Rachel, 1894-1942.
Prayer for a child / by Rachel Field ; pictures by Elizabeth Orton
Jones.— Diamond anniversary ed.
p. cm.
Originally published: New York Macmillan, 1944.
ISBN-13: 978-0-689-87356-0 (ISBN-10: 0-689-87356-5)
1. Bedtime prayers. 2. Children—Prayer-books and
devotions—English. I. Jones, Elizabeth Orton, 1910– II. Title.
BV283.B43F54 2004
242'.82—dc22   2004005259

ISBN 978-1-4169-9610-1 (unjacketed edition)

FOR HANNAH

PRAYER FOR A CHILD

Bless this milk and bless this bread.
Bless this soft and waiting bed
Where I presently shall be
Wrapped in sweet security.
Through the darkness, through the night
Let no danger come to fright
My sleep till morning once again
Beckons at the window pane.
Bless the toys whose shapes I know,
The shoes that take me to and fro
Up and down and everywhere.
Bless my little painted chair.
Bless the lamplight, bless the fire,
Bless the hands that never tire
In their loving care of me.
Bless my friends and family.
Bless my Father and my Mother
And keep us close to one another.
Bless other children, far and near,
And keep them safe and free from fear.
So let me sleep and let me wake
In peace and health, for Jesus' sake.
                                    Amen.

less this milk and bless this bread.

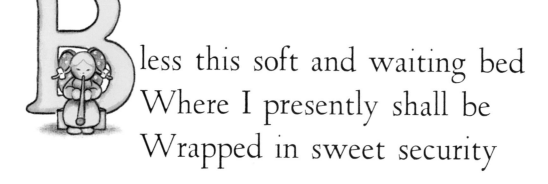

Bless this soft and waiting bed
Where I presently shall be
Wrapped in sweet security

Through the darkness, through the night
Let no danger come to fright
My sleep till morning once again
Beckons at the window pane

less the toys whose shapes I know

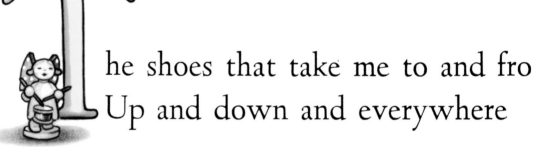

The shoes that take me to and fro
Up and down and everywhere

less my little painted chair

less the lamplight, bless the fire

less the hands that never tire
In their loving care of me

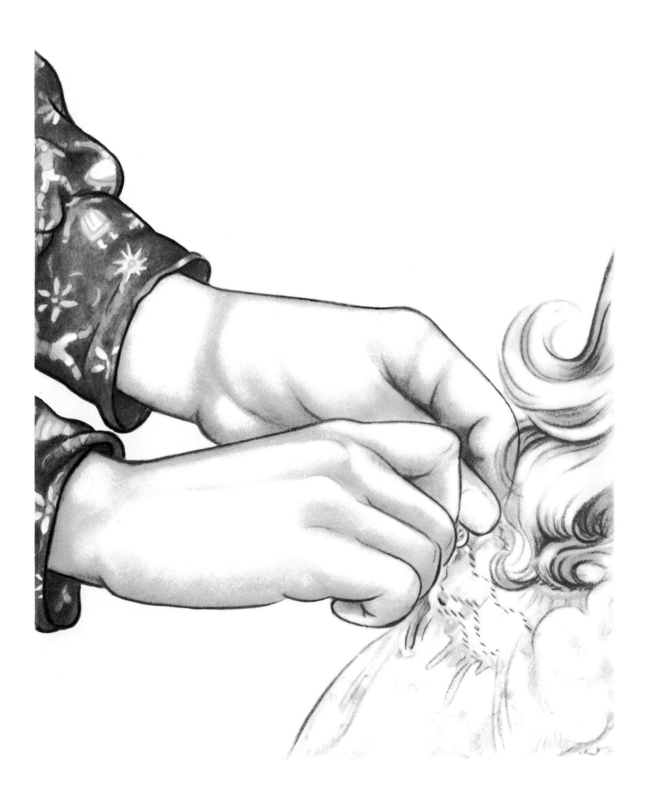

less my friends and family

less my Father and my Mother
And keep us close to one another

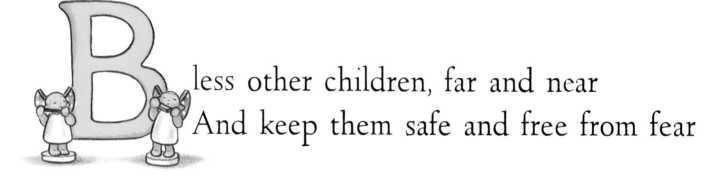

Bless other children, far and near
And keep them safe and free from fear

So let me sleep and let me wake
In peace and health, for Jesus' sake

men